Leaders of the American Revolution

John Adams

American Patriot

Leaders of the American Revolution

Thomas Paine and the Fight for Liberty

John Adams American Patriot

Paul Revere Messenger for Freedom

Betsy Ross A Flag for a New Nation

Benedict Arnold Hero and Traitor

Alexander Hamilton Framer of the Constitution

Molly Pitcher Heroine of the War for Independence

Nathan Hale Courageous Spy

John Paul Jones American Naval Hero

George Washington America's Leader in War and Peace

Leaders of the American Revolution

John Adams

American Patriot

Samuel Willard Crompton

CHELSEA HOUSE
PUBLISHERS
A Haights Cross Communications Company ®
Philadelphia

CHELSEA HOUSE PUBLISHERS
VP, NEW PRODUCT DEVELOPMENT Sally Cheney
DIRECTOR OF PRODUCTION Kim Shinners
CREATIVE MANAGER Takeshi Takahashi
MANUFACTURING MANAGER Diann Grasse

Staff for John Adams
EXECUTIVE EDITOR Lee Marcott
EDITORIAL ASSISTANT Carla Greenberg
PRODUCTION EDITOR Bonnie Cohen
PHOTO EDITOR Sarah Bloom
COVER AND INTERIOR DESIGNER Keith Trego
LAYOUT 21st Century Publishing and Communications, Inc.

A Haights Cross Communications ✦ Company ®

www.chelseahouse.com

First Printing

9 8 7 6 5 4 3 2 1

Library of Congress Cataloging-in-Publication Data

Crompton, Samuel Willard.
    John Adams: American patriot/Samuel Willard Compton.
       p. cm.—(Leaders of the american revolution)
    Includes bibliographical references and index.
    ISBN 0-7910-8620-8 (hardcover)
1. Adams, Johm 1735–1826—Juvenile literature. 2. Presidents—United States—
biography—Juvenile literature. I. Title. II. Series.
E322.C94 2005
973.4'4'092—dc2

                                                    2005001575

All links and web addresses were checked and verified to be correct at the time of publication.
Because of the dynamic nature of the web, some addresses and links may have changed since
publication and may no longer be valid.

Contents

The Trial

It was the third of December, in the year 1770. A young Boston lawyer stepped forward to defend eight men accused of murder.

John Adams was the lawyer. The eight men were British soldiers, accused of murdering five Americans. No one could argue about the event. Everyone knew that five

Americans were dead. The question was, had they been murdered? Or had the seven British soldiers acted in self-defense?

John Adams had been asked to defend these men. John Adams was a patriot who believed that the presence of British soldiers in Boston was wrong and the heavy taxes Britain had placed on its colonies were unjust. But he also believed in the right of every man accused to have a lawyer and a fair trial. So he had agreed to take on the unpopular and even dangerous task of representing the British soldiers.

John Adams began his defense by describing what had happened on the night of March 5, 1770. It had been a cold winter night. Toward evening, a large group of Bostonians had approached the Customs House and taunted the soldier on guard. He stood outside the Customs House with a musket on one shoulder. He was there to defend the building where taxes and duties were paid, as a demonstration of the strength and importance of the British government.

But the Bostonians resented the presence of the soldiers, and the Customs House was a symbol of the hated taxes they were being forced to pay. They threw snowballs at the soldier. They called him "Lobster

John Adams first gained fame as a young attorney charged with defending eight British soldiers accused of murder in the Boston Massacre of 1770.

Back" and "Bloody Back" (both names referred to the red color of his British uniform).

When he could take it no more, the soldier ran inside and rang a large bell. The bell sounded through the streets of Boston, and seven British soldiers, led by Captain Preston, came running. Soon there were eight men with muskets and one captain to lead them, facing down the hostile and angry colonists.

The number of colonists gathered in the street quickly increased, as well. Soon there were one hundred, then two hundred Bostonians. They had already thrown snowballs. Now they began to pack and throw balls of ice.

John Adams explained all this to the court. Then he defended the British soldiers who had fired into the crowd. He explained that there was great noise and confusion, and then the British soldiers thought their captain called out the order "Fire." More likely, he called, "Whatever you do, don't fire," but the crowd was too large and the noise too great for him to be heard. So the British soldiers fired and soon there were five dead bodies in the street.

Everyone was horrified by what had happened. British soldiers had never fired at colonists before. More people might have been murdered, had not leaders on both sides intervened, preventing further bloodshed.

IN DEFENSE OF THE FACTS

John Adams clearly and carefully explained the events

of that night—the night of the Boston Massacre of 1770. In his defense of the eight soldiers, he explained that under British law a man is presumed innocent until he is found guilty. He reminded the members of the jury that the crowd had taunted and even attacked the soldiers. He told them that one soldier had been hit with a club before the shooting began. And finally, John Adams told the men of the jury (there were no women), "Facts are stubborn things and whatever may be our wishes, our inclinations, or the dictums of our passions, they cannot alter the state of facts and evidence."[1]

John Adams's words sound strange to us, because he used the more formal language of the eighteenth century. But his idea that judges and jury members should not let their feelings overcome the facts remains clear. If the British soldiers were innocent, then the court must let them go, despite their own personal reactions to the incident.

Like any good lawyer, Adams paused at the end. He watched as the members of the jury went away. They went into a separate room and stayed there for two hours. While the members of the jury debated, Adams had to wait. So did the eight British soldiers who were accused of murder.

The clock ticked on the wall. Occasional bells were heard from the outside world. But the court was like a closed place, a place where time had stopped.

Finally, the members of the jury returned. When asked, they said that they had reached their decision. Of the eight British soldiers, they found six to be wholly innocent. The remaining two were found guilty of manslaughter, a lesser crime than murder. These two men were to have their thumbs branded with iron-hot markers as punishment. Not one of the eight soldiers was found guilty of murder.

Some colonists were upset. They thought justice had been denied. They blamed John Adams.

John Adams was hurt. He supported those who protested the unjust taxes placed on the colonies. He felt that the presence of British soldiers policing Boston harbor was wrong. And he wanted to be popular. But he had done his duty. He had done what he thought was right.

The trial following the Boston Massacre defined John Adams, both the man he was and the man he would become. He would continue to work hard, to take on difficult challenges, even to adopt unpopular positions if he believed in the justice and rightness of his cause. Adams was a passionate defender of liberty, and his efforts to protect and preserve America would shape his life.

Test Your Knowledge

1 Who were the eight men John Adams represented in the trial following the Boston Massacre?

a. Members of the Sons of Liberty.

b. Patriots accused of plotting revolution against Britain.

c. British soldiers.

d. Bostonians who had attacked soldiers guarding the Customs House.

2 Why did Adams agree to take the case?

a. At the time, he still was a strong supporter of the British crown and its representatives in the colonies.

b. He believed that all men had a right to legal representation and a fair trial.

c. He was eager to expand his legal practice and hoped that more Loyalists would hire him after the trial.

d. He believed that the soldiers had been wrongly accused and were innocent of the crime.

3 What were the key points of Adams's defense?

a. The mob had taunted and attacked the soldiers first.

b. The soldiers thought their captain had ordered them to fire.

c. The noise and confusion of the night made the events unclear.

d. All of the above.

4 What was the jury's verdict?

   a. All of the soldiers were found not guilty.

   b. The eight soldiers were found guilty of murder.

   c. Six were found innocent, while two were found guilty of manslaughter.

   d. The soldiers were acquitted, but their captain was found guilty.

5 How did the public view Adams after the trial?

   a. He was criticized for defending the soldiers.

   b. He was praised for his brilliant defense.

   c. He was arrested for aiding the enemy.

   d. None of the above.

ANSWERS: 1. c; 2. b; 3. d; 4. c; 5. a

Yankee Youth

John Adams was born in Braintree, Massachusetts, on October 19, 1735. His father was also named John Adams and his mother was Susannah Boylston.

The Adams family had been in New England for nearly 100 years. The first members of the Adams clan to settle in the colonies had arrived from England in 1639. They were

John Adams spent much of his life in this home in Massachusetts.

Puritans—Christians who had attempted to purify the Church of England, first in their homeland and then in America, by stripping away what they viewed as religious excesses and seeking instead a simpler form of worship—worship as it had been carried out in the time of Christ.

The Adams family did well in Massachusetts. The first Adams to arrive is believed to have had nearly 80 grandchildren.

John Adams grew up in a five-room, saltbox-style house in Braintree. Much is known about his youth, in part because Adams often wrote and spoke about his childhood. He always spoke very highly of his father, praising him as the sort of person who contributed to making the colony of Massachusetts so vital and prosperous. His father was a leading member of the Braintree church and a skilled man capable of fixing nearly anything—a talent that was greatly needed in New England in the 1730s and 1740s.

John Adams was rather small for his age, but what he lacked in size he made up for in intelligence. From an early age, he loved books and spent many hours reading about Greek and Roman heroes, as well as the great men of English history. Adams dreamed of becoming a soldier, but his small size and family plans conspired against this. His parents had high aspirations for their intelligent young son. They wanted him to go to Harvard College.

A COLLEGE EDUCATION

Harvard was founded in the 1630s, and had been a presence in the colony of Massachusetts for as long as the Adams family had. Harvard was one of the few colleges in the American colonies—there were only two others, Yale College in Connecticut and the College of William and Mary in Virginia—and it was the place where successful, ambitious and wealthy young men in Massachusetts went to be educated.

The minister in Braintree tutored John Adams and he passed the exams to enter Harvard. Young men attended college at an earlier age in the eighteenth century (and women did not attend college at all). Adams entered Harvard at the age of 16 and graduated at twenty. Years later, Adams described this time as one of the best of his life. He loved to learn and he was fascinated by the people he met at Harvard.

John Adams graduated from Harvard College in 1755. This was the year that the French and Indian War began. Britain and its American colonies went to war with France over the right to territory in North America. The war caused much excitement in the colonies and young John Adams wanted, more than anything, to join.

However, Adams's hope of becoming a soldier would once more be shattered. Adams was not very strong physically and his small size made recruiters reject him. Perhaps more significantly, Adams came from a family that had played a leading role in their town—a family that did not wish its son to throw himself away on a military life.

So John Adams stayed at home. He did not go to war, but later in life, during the Revolution, he would meet and work with many of those who did serve in the French and Indian War. One of them was George Washington, who was only three years older than John Adams.

In 1755, John Adams rode from Braintree to Worcester, Massachusetts, to begin his career as a teacher. This was an honorable profession, but one that did not pay very well. Adams taught for about two years and then decided to practice law.

There were no law schools in the eighteenth century. Instead, a young man went to the office of an established attorney and clerked for him, writing out documents in long hand and serving as an assistant while learning as much about the business of law as possible. There were no computers or fax machines in those days and much of a young man's time was spent copying and recopying documents. Within two years, John Adams had served his apprenticeship and was ready to open his own law office.

Adams's first job was as a teacher in a one-room schoolhouse similar to this one. After two years, he left teaching to practice law.

FINDING LOVE

Just as Adams was beginning his career as a lawyer, an event happened that would further transform his life. He met a young woman who would prove to be the love of his life.

Her name was Abigail Smith. She lived in
Weymouth, Massachusetts, not far from John Adams's
home in Braintree. The two met for the first time in
1761. It was not love at first sight for either of them.
She found him to be short and talkative, boastful and
impressed with himself. He found a woman who was
even shorter than he was, with rosy cheeks and a
friendly manner to everyone but him.

Courtship

Courtship in the eighteenth century was very different
from today. Families, especially parents, were more
involved in the matter. A father and mother wanted to
know the young man who paid court to their daughter.
The father and mother wanted to "sound out" the young
man, to make sure he was suitable.

People married at about the same age they do now.
Young men married in their mid- to late twenties and
young women in their late teens and early twenties.
Young couples usually had children as soon as possible and families of eight to ten children were not
considered unusual. In part this was because most
Americans lived on farms, and large families, with

But they met again, and again, and gradually they began to see beyond the first impressions. The Yankee youth came courting a year or two later. Courtship was an involved ritual in those days. Even a serious and ambitious man like John Adams had to prove to the woman's family that he was worthy of their daughter. He had to show them, through his actions, that he loved their daughter and that he would do well for her in the future.

many children who could work on the farm, were seen as an asset.

We know more about John Adams and Abigail Smith's courtship than is usual because they wrote long letters to each other. They used Roman and Greek names in their correspondence. He called her Diana, for the Roman goddess, and she called him Lysander, for the Spartan hero. Their courtship was longer than average, partly because John Adams underwent a painful inoculation for smallpox in 1764. He spent weeks in recovery, pushing the wedding date back by several months. Perhaps their long courtship was a good thing, because once married, they stayed very much in love for the rest of their lives.

It is fortunate that many of the letters that Abigail Smith and John Adams exchanged have survived. Their developing friendship gives us a wonderful look at courtship and romance in the eighteenth century.

Abigail Smith's mother did not like John Adams. She thought he was below her daughter and she wanted Abigail to marry a man with a higher station in life. But the courtship continued and a month before the wedding, John Adams wrote to the girl he intended to marry: "You who had always softened and warmed my heart, shall restore my benevolence as well as my health and tranquility of mind. You shall polish and refine my sentiments of life and manners, banish all the unsocial and ill natured particles in my composition, and form me to that happy temper, that can reconcile a quick discernment with a perfect candor."[2]

This letter was forward-looking. John Adams had predicted what marriage would mean to him. Throughout their long lives together, Abigail Smith would give to John Adams the gentleness he needed, and he would give to her his strength.

The wedding took place in October 1764. Adams and his new bride moved into the house next to his parents' home. His father was now dead, but his mother

Adams married Abigail Smith in October 1764. Her mother argued against the marriage, wanting her daughter to marry someone more successful.

lived in the same saltbox home in which Adams had spent his childhood. She and her new daughter-in-law became fast and good friends, much to John Adams's pleasure. By the year 1765, his life was happy and full. He was married, living in his own home, and making a good living as a lawyer. He had fulfilled most of the hopes of his early life, except the one of being a soldier. Never would he actually wear a uniform or fight in battle, but he would become one of America's greatest patriots in the struggle that was to come.

Test Your Knowledge

1 Where was John Adams born?

a. London, England.

b. Williamsburg, Virginia.

c. Albany, New York.

d. Braintree, Massachusetts.

2 Where was Adams educated?

a. At Harvard College.

b. At the College of William and Mary.

c. At a school operated by his father.

d. At Oxford University.

3 What role did Adams play in the French and Indian War?

a. He served under George Washington.

b. He was a commander of the Massachusetts militia.

c. He was a spy, operating behind enemy lines.

d. He did not serve in the war.

4 What was Adams's first job?

a. Lawyer.

b. Teacher.

c. Doctor.

d. Surveyor.

5 Who was Abigail Smith?

   a. Adams's first client.

   b. Adams's favorite sister-in-law.

   c. The woman Adams married.

   d. A wealthy Boston seamstress.

ANSWERS: 1. d; 2. a; 3. d; 4. b; 5. c

Young Revolutionary

T he Stamp Act changed John Adams's life. He became a firm Patriot because of this tax, which was put on the American colonies in 1765.

King George III was ruler of both Britain and its empire overseas. King George meant well. He was an honest, hard-working man. But he did not understand his American colonies or the colonists themselves.

King George and the British Parliament believed that the Americans should pay taxes directly to Britain. They had never done this before. All taxes in the past had been raised by the individual colonies. But King George believed that the American colonists owed something to Britain, because Britain had defeated France in the French and Indian War. This war had made the American colonists safe and had created huge debts for Britain. It was only right, King George and the Parliament stated, that the American colonists should help share the cost of the war through taxes.

In 1765, the Stamp Act went into effect. Under this new law, colonists had to pay for stamps, which they bought at a British customs office, stamps to make their documents legal. Wills, deeds, newspapers, and other documents all had to have the stamps to make them legal and official.

Americans from every colony hated the Stamp Act. But it was in Massachusetts that resistance to the act was most clearly demonstrated. Lawyers like John Adams and merchants like John Hancock felt that this tax would burden them in an unfair way. But even more importantly, colonists believed that this new tax went against British law and tradition. Soon people were using the expression "No Taxation without Representation" to demonstrate their views.[3]

POLITICAL WRITER

This was a turning point in John Adams's life. He had a wife and home to support, and he already had his first child, a daughter named Abigail. He could easily have said that his first duty was to his home and family. But John Adams was a lawyer, through and through. After studying English law, he had come to the conclusion that the Stamp Act was not only an unjust tax, but was also a violation of English law. In 1766, at the age of 30, he wrote one of his most important political essays, "A Dissertation on the Canon and the Feudal Law." It was reprinted in England under the title "The True Sentiments of America."

From this first major work, we gain an understanding of John Adams's thoughts. He was no radical. John Adams did not approve of mob rule or of people taking the law into their own hands. The law was, to him, a very sacred thing. According to Adams, the American colonists had no need for mob action because the

British constitution defended their interests. They could not be taxed because British law protected their rights. In his essay, he noted, "Government is a plain, simple, intelligent thing, founded in nature and reason, quite comprehensible by common sense."[4]

This was, and remained, one of the keystones of John Adams's thinking. Government and law were available to all, and existed for the benefit of all.

John Adams's new political writing was hailed by many people. They saw him as the successor to James Otis, another Massachusetts lawyer, who had opposed another British act four years earlier. James Otis was slowly losing his mind and was less and less able to lead the Patriot cause in Massachusetts. Now it appeared as if John Adams would be the perfect replacement.

The Stamp Act was not defeated by John Adams, however. It was defeated by his second cousin, Samuel Adams, who did believe in the use of the mobs. In 1765, Samuel Adams organized the Sons of Liberty in Boston. They harassed and sometimes attacked British officers who sold the hated stamps. A few houses were burned. The result was that the British Parliament revoked the Stamp Act in 1766.

The colonists celebrated the decision, going so far as to praise King George III for his wisdom in taking action following colonial protests. This shows that the colonists were not eager, at least in 1765, to break away from England. Instead, they wanted England to acknowledge their rights, rights that came from the British constitution itself.

With the Stamp Act crisis at an end, John Adams went back to work. He had a growing family to support. He and Abigail now had three children— Abigail, John Quincy, and Charles—and he needed to make money. He went out on the riding circuit as a lawyer. He argued cases as far away as Maine and New Hampshire.

In 1768, John and Abigail Adams moved their young family from Braintree to Boston. This was a big move. They left a village of a few hundred people and moved to a city of about 16,000. The move was necessary because John Adams had now become the most active lawyer in Boston, and he needed to be in the city to better serve his clients and better observe events as they happened. Coincidentally, the family move happened at the same time that British soldiers first arrived in Boston.

A CLIMATE OF CRISIS

By 1768, King George III had declared a new set of tax laws. They put taxes on things like paper, paint, glass, and tea. To make sure that these taxes were collected, King George sent over two British regiments. These soldiers increased the population of Boston by more than a thousand, and because there were no army barracks to house them, the soldiers had to live in the homes of Bostonians. The soldiers were housed, or "quartered," in the homes of the colonists under the terms of the Quartering Act.

Many Bostonians were upset at the Quartering Act. They were forced to house and even to feed the British soldiers under their roofs. The Adams family was not required to quarter any soldiers, and Adams's busy law practice initially prevented him from focusing too closely on the unrest and anger the Quartering Act was sparking in Boston. But the events of March 5, 1770, changed things for him, and for many other Bostonians as well.

As we saw in the first chapter, in response to the harassment of an angry crowd, eight British soldiers fired into a crowd of Bostonians, five of whom were killed. The very next day, John Adams was asked to defend the British soldiers. He knew that to do so would cost him popularity in Boston. People might even stop using him as their lawyer. But he believed so firmly in the concepts of British law and British liberty that he agreed on the spot to represent the soldiers.

John Adams spent the second half of 1770 preparing the case. He had to argue two cases—one in defense of their commanding officer, Captain Preston, and another in defense of the eight soldiers. John Adams prepared with great skill, and he won a complete acquittal for Captain Preston. Then he defended the eight soldiers and did so well that only two of them were found guilty of manslaughter (not murder). The other six soldiers were found acquitted.

For the rest of his life, John Adams looked back with pride and satisfaction on these cases. He had stepped forward, done the unpopular thing, and he had shown that American colonists used British law and British rights in an equal, even-handed way. This was a great victory, a victory won by doing what was right, rather than what was easy.

At the same time, the two court cases of 1770 pushed John Adams into being more of a revolutionary. He would never change his ideas about mob action and violence. He would always be against these. But in the two or three years after the Boston Massacre, John Adams became increasingly convinced that the American colonies would eventually have to separate from the mother country of Britain.

A GROWING DISSATISFACTION

For about two years after the Massacre, Boston was fairly quiet. Then, in 1773, a fleet of ships carrying tea arrived in Boston Harbor. There was nothing revolutionary about this. Tea ships came and went all the time. But a new, three-penny tax on each pound of tea had recently been passed and the colonists were furious. They had resisted the Stamp Act in 1765. They had used every means to avoid buying paper, paint, glass, and tea in the past. Now there was a new tax.

John Adams did not play a role in the tea tax matter. His cousin, Samuel Adams, did. Samuel Adams organized the Sons of Liberty in Boston and they stopped the ship captains from landing their tea. When the ship captains refused to give up and sail away, Samuel Adams led hundreds of Bostonians down to the wharf on the night of December 16, 1773. Dressed up as Mohawk Indians, the Bostonians boarded the ships

John Adams's cousin, Samuel Adams, organized the Sons of Liberty.

and heaved all of the chests of tea into the harbor. This was a stunning example of mob rule and the power of revolutionary action.

John Adams did not play any part in the Boston Tea Party, but he approved of it and understood its significance. He wrote in his diary: "This destruction of the tea is so bold, so daring, so firm, intrepid and inflexible, and it must have so important consequences and so lasting, that I can't but consider it as an epoch in history!"[5]

Adams was increasingly convinced that Britain would not respect the rights of the colonists until it was forced to do so. By the early part of 1774, John Adams had become one of the three or four most important Patriot leaders in Boston.

In the spring of 1774, Bostonians learned of the consequences of the Boston Tea Party. King George III was outraged over the destruction of the tea. He ordered that the port of Boston be closed. He also ordered that all town meetings in the colony of Massachusetts be suspended. Finally, he announced that Salem, not Boston, would be the future capital city of Massachusetts. Of the three declarations, this last one was the hardest to enforce. All these declarations were to remain in force until Boston paid for the tea its people had destroyed in 1773.

With their port closed, Bostonians went without work. Some of them went hungry. John Adams's law

Events like the Boston Tea Party prompted King George III to order the closing of Boston's port.

practice suffered. So did the businesses of men like John Hancock and Paul Revere. Among all these men, however, there was a stubborn decision to resist. They and their fellow Bostonians would never yield to what they believed was British tyranny.

Boston might have slowly starved if it were not for the other colonies. People in Virginia and South Carolina loaded food and supplies on wagons and sent them north to Boston. Virtually all of the colonies agreed that Boston must not yield to the British punishments.

FIRST CONTINENTAL CONGRESS

As a major gesture of unity, the colonies agreed to hold a meeting of an inter-colonial legislature. Representatives from 12 of the 13 colonies (Georgia did not participate) were sent to Philadelphia in the autumn of 1774.

John Adams, Samuel Adams, and Robert Treat Paine were selected as the delegates from Massachusetts. They gathered in Boston and went south in August 1774. What greeted them in Philadelphia was a busy, prosperous city and a new spirit of unity among the colonists.

Although he knew Massachusetts, Maine, and New Hampshire well, John Adams had never before left New England. He and his fellow delegates loved Philadelphia. Its broad, well-lit streets and handsome houses were even more impressive than those of Boston. In fact, Philadelphia was one of the largest cities of the British Empire, second only to London.

In Philadelphia, John Adams met many men with whom he would work for the next decade. He met the Virginian delegate George Washington and the South Carolinian Henry Laurens. Adams was very impressed with his fellow delegates. They came from different parts of the colonies, but they shared a belief in freedom and resistance to British tyranny.

The First Continental Congress, as it was called, resolved that the colonies would continue to support Boston. No matter what actions the British Parliament took, the delegates were determined that Boston must not submit. The delegates to the First Continental Congress also agreed to meet in May of the following year.

THE WARNING IS SPREAD

When the Congress ended, John Adams returned to his family, which now included four children. A fifth child, a daughter, had died about one year after her birth. The sorrow over this loss was so deep that John Adams did not speak of it for many years.

The winter of 1774–1775 was a tense time. There were now about 4,000 British troops in Boston, and their presence meant that the city had a total population of about 20,000. There was anger and resentment on both sides, and things only got worse as spring approached.

In April 1775, the British governor of Massachusetts, Thomas Gage, received instructions from the king.

Boston Then, Boston Now

Today, Boston is a favored tourist destination. Millions of people come to walk the Freedom Trail, to browse in Faneuil Hall's marketplace, and to retrace the steps of the revolutionaries of 1775. More than 2.5 million people live in Boston and its suburbs, making it the largest city in New England.

In 1775, when the Revolution began, Boston was a city of 16,000 townspeople and 4,000 British troops. The 20,000 people were crowded onto a narrow peninsula that was connected to the mainland by a strip of land called "The Neck." Anyone who went to Boston by land crossed over this narrow neck (today the land around the neck has been filled in and Boston is much larger).

On the evening of April 18, 1775, Paul Revere waited at Charlestown, just across the Charles River from

George III told his governor to send troops out into the countryside and to seize the muskets and powder of the American colonists. Governor Gage knew this would be a tricky thing to pull off, but he sent out one thousand soldiers on the night of April 18, 1775.

On that same night, Paul Revere waited for a sign. He was standing on the Charlestown side of the Charles

Boston. He waited to see whether one or two lamps were hung in the belfry of the Old North Church. If it was one lamp, then the British were going "by land," meaning by way of the neck. If two lamps were hung, then the British were going by sea, meaning that they would travel by boat across the Charles River. When Paul Revere saw two lamps, he knew that the British were coming, and he rode away in the night, alerting the people of Middlesex County.

Boston today is much larger than in 1775, but one can still enjoy parts of the old city. Walking the cobblestone streets of the Old North End and breathing the salt air near the docks, one can still imagine what it must have been like to live in Boston more than two centuries ago.

River. When he saw two lights shining from the belfry of the Old North Church, he knew that the British were coming by way of the Charles River instead of by land. Revere jumped onto a horse and rode west, spreading the news that British troops were on the march, headed in that direction.

Paul Revere was captured by the British near Lexington, but other dispatch riders carried the warning. By morning, there were 70 militiamen on Lexington Green. As the British troops advanced, it was clear that there might be a fight. The British commander rode out in front of his men and shouted, "Lay down your arms, you damned rebels, and disperse!"[6]

The Massachusetts militia began to move away. They did not lay down their arms, but they started to leave Lexington Green. As they did, someone fired a shot. No one knows who fired that first shot. But that single shot erupted into what would become known as the Battle of Lexington. Within minutes, the British troops claimed victory. Ten Americans were dead or wounded. The others escaped to fight later. The British gave three cheers and advanced through Lexington on their way to Concord.

John Adams missed both the Battle of Lexington and the Battle of Concord, which took place on the same day. He was in Braintree, working on his family farm. When he heard the news, Adams rushed to Cambridge, where colonial militia were gathering. He was elated by the news of the battle and believed that all would be for the best. He wrote a long letter to Abigail, describing the scene of the battles and the way in which the colonial militia won the day. Only a careful reader could hear the disappointment in his words. As in his youth, John Adams was a man of words, of committees, and of resolutions. He still was not the soldier he had once hoped to become.

Two weeks later, John Adams, his cousin Samuel Adams, and their friend John Hancock traveled to Philadelphia to serve as Massachusetts's delegates to the Second Continental Congress.

Test Your Knowledge

I What British action inspired Adams to become a Patriot?

   a. The tax on tea.

   b. The Stamp Act.

   c. The Boston Massacre.

   d. The attack at Lexington.

2 In his essay "A Dissertation on the Canon and the Feudal Law," what ideas did Adams express?

   a. Colonists did not need to form mobs to take action.

   b. The British constitution guaranteed the rights of the colonists.

   c. Government was a plain, simple, intelligent thing.

   d. All of the above.

3 Why were British soldiers sent to Boston?

   a. To ensure that taxes were collected.

   b. To claim the city for the British king.

   c. To prepare for an attack against French settlements in Canada.

   d. To train the colonial militia.

4 Why did Adams travel to Philadelphia in the autumn of 1774?

    a. He had been hired by a client in Pennsylvania.

    b. The British had ordered him to leave Boston.

    c. He was serving as a delegate to the First Continental Congress.

    d. None of the above.

5 When Adams learned of the battles at Lexington and Concord, how did he respond?

    a. He enlisted in the Massachusetts militia.

    b. He insisted that his family leave their farm and travel with him to Philadelphia.

    c. He was excited at the news of the battle and wrote home describing the battles and the bravery of the colonial militia.

    d. He urged the British to surrender.

ANSWERS: 1. b; 2. d; 3. a; 4. c; 5. c

Leading
the Way to
Independence

John Adams and his fellow delegates arrived in Philadelphia on May 10, 1775. Only six months had passed since they were there at the First Continental Congress. Now they were leading members of the Second Continental Congress. Much had changed in those six months. The American colonies were now at war with Great Britain.

Soon after he arrived in Philadelphia, John Adams made the acquaintance of Benjamin Franklin. The two men's careers would be intertwined over the next decade. Franklin was then one of the American colonies' most famous citizens. Born in Boston in 1706, he had moved to Philadelphia as a young man and made his fortune in the printing and writing of newspapers and almanacs. Initially, Franklin had not supported the idea of independence from Great Britain, but he had gradually changed his position. The same could not be said of many other members of the Second Continental Congress.

John Adams had an impatient nature. He was not accustomed to waiting and allowing events to take their own course. He believed that the time had come for a formal declaration of independence from Great Britain. But many of his fellow delegates did not agree.

One of the delegates opposed to independence was John Dickinson of Pennsylvania. A farmer, a lawyer, and a man of deep, careful thought, Dickinson believed it would be better for the American colonies to make peace with Great Britain.

John Adams was usually a careful and thoughtful man in public. In private, he was far more open in

While serving as a delegate to the Second Continental Congress in Philadelphia, Adams met Benjamin Franklin. The two men's careers would be intertwined for the next decade.

expressing his opinions and feelings, especially in letters to his wife and friends. In 1775, John Adams sent a letter to a friend in which he described John Dickinson as a "piddling genius," an expression clearly meant as an insult.[7] Unfortunately, the letter, along with others, fell into British hands. The British published the letter in one of their newspapers, and soon it was known to everyone that John Adams of Massachusetts had insulted John Dickinson of Pennsylvania. The publication of the letter was no doubt intended to embarrass Adams and drive a wedge into the Continental Congress, and for a time, it succeeded.

A SIGN OF UNITY

While Adams was dealing with the fallout from the publication of his insulting letter, he won praise for a major success. In June 1775, just one month into the meetings of the Second Continental Congress, he stood up and recommended that Congress choose George Washington of Virginia as the new commander-in-chief of the Continental Army. People were surprised that Adams, as a New Englander, would nominate a Virginian to the important post, but

Adams knew that the colonies must work together. To avoid the appearance of the conflict being simply between New England and Britain, Adams believed that choosing a Virginian (from the largest of the American colonies) as commander of the army would promote unity and reduce rivalries between the colonies. Since so many of the militiamen were from New England, it was very important to have a southerner as the army's leader to ensure that the army be more clearly representative of the unity of the colonies.

Adams's motion was seconded by his cousin, Samuel Adams, and passed the Congress. George Washington became the commander-in-chief of the Continental Army.

John Adams was happy serving as a delegate to the Continental Congress, but his wife was not happy with his long absences. She had to raise the children and manage the family farm entirely on her own, and she felt his absence strongly. In letter after letter, she praised his efforts in Congress, but also reminded him of how much he was needed at home. His letters back reminded her that he could not leave this important post. In fact, he was soon given an even higher position, as

Chairman of the Board of War. Here he was, a man who had often dreamed of being a soldier and never had the chance. Instead, he was leader of the war effort in the Continental Congress!

As was typical, John Adams did not shrink from duty. He soon learned more about guns, gunpowder, cannons, and ships than most of his fellow delegates in Philadelphia. He made recommendations about how Congress should create a navy and provide for the defense of the 13 colonies (they were not yet 13 states). Some of his recommendations were turned down, but he succeeded in persuading his fellow delegates of the need for the colonies to develop a fighting force at sea, and in November 1775 Congress created the first small beginnings of what would become the American navy.

In December 1775, John Adams was able to go home for three weeks. Even though he had only been away for six months, he found the family changed. His children had grown older and more intelligent. His wife had become more confident in her role as the head of the family while he was gone. And the war, with its many battles near and around Boston, was very much in evidence.

THE BOARD OF WAR

John Adams enjoyed his brief homecoming, but he was soon off for Philadelphia once more. As the Chairman of the Board of War, his presence at the meetings of the Congress was vital. When he arrived, Adams found that the morale of the delegates was very low. They were discouraged by the first year of the war, and the meager results that had been accomplished. There were pessimists in the Congress who felt it was impossible to ever defeat Great Britain.

Adams did his best to answer these pessimistic feelings, but nothing he did had as much effect as the publication of a 46-page pamphlet called *Common Sense*. Written by Thomas Paine, an Englishman who had just moved to America, *Common Sense* called for a complete and final break with Great Britain. Thomas Paine told his readers that Britain was powerful indeed, but that the colonists had the power of right on their side. So what if England had a great army and a great navy? The colonists were fighting for the cause of freedom. They would prevail.

John Adams and thousands of others read *Common Sense*. Most people who read it were impressed by the power of the words and the way they were used.

John Adams sent a copy of *Common Sense* to Abigail. He praised the words and the eloquence of the pamphlet, but he also commented that Thomas Paine was much better at "tearing down" governments than he was at building them. What would replace the rule of Great Britain?

It is clear that John and Abigail Adams were not radicals. They loved the world into which they had been born. They loved the quiet independence enjoyed by Americans who ran their own farms and shops, but they did not love the implied violence of radical revolution, which they heard in Thomas Paine's writing.

While they had a respect for tradition and a careful approach to planning and politics, John and Abigail Adams were ahead of many Americans when it came to relations between the two sexes. In one of her letters to her husband, Abigail Adams wrote, "I desire you would remember the ladies, and be more favorable to them than your ancestors. Do not put such unlimited power into the hands of husbands. . . . Remember all men would be tyrants if they could."[8]

John Adams wrote back in good humor. He pointed out that women generally had the upper hand in matters at home and that it was important for men to have the upper hand in society. Though he wrote in a light spirit, John Adams was not able to support the idea of equality between men and women. That was an idea whose time had not yet come.

DECLARING INDEPENDENCE

The push for independence was now strong. In the spring of 1776, John Adams and his fellow delegates learned that George Washington, the new commander-in-chief, had forced the British out of Boston. This was the greatest victory the Patriots had yet won, and the hearts of the men in Philadelphia were lifted.

On June 7, 1776, Richard Lee of Virginia rose to make a motion in the Continental Congress. His words were the ones John Adams longed to hear and the ones that John Dickinson and others most feared. Richard Lee called for a declaration of the freedom and complete independence of the 13 colonies.

John Adams was elated. He, Benjamin Franklin, Thomas Jefferson, and two other men were chosen as a committee to draft the new declaration.

Born in Virginia in 1743, Thomas Jefferson was eight years younger than John Adams. While Adams and Jefferson shared a belief in the need

Adams was chosen as one of the delegates charged with drafting the Declaration of Independence. The committee also included Benjamin Franklin, Thomas Jefferson, Robert Livingston, and Roger Sherman.

for independence from Britain, they were very different men. Jefferson had little of the stern nature of John Adams and also lacked his way with other people. But Jefferson was highly educated. He had studied the classics, just as John Adams had, and had a greater ability with his pen. So, when it came time to decide how to write the declaration, John Adams and three other committee members agreed to let Thomas Jefferson write the first draft entirely on his own. This was a great compliment to pay to anyone, but, as it turned out, Thomas Jefferson was worthy.

Jefferson spent about ten days by himself. He then brought to the committee his declaration. This was a remarkable document, written in Jefferson's precise and elegant hand. The document began: "When, in the course of human events, it becomes necessary for one people to dissolve the political bonds which have connected them with another, and to assume, among the powers of the earth, the separate and equal station to which the laws of nature and of nature's God entitle them. . . ."

Jefferson's inspiring words outlined the reasons why the colonists felt it necessary to break their political bonds with Britain. He described how King George III had trampled on the liberties of Americans, which derived from the liberties of Englishmen. For these reasons, Jefferson wrote, the 13 colonies declared themselves free and independent of Great Britain.

The words were Jefferson's and he deserves all credit for them. But the ideas behind the words were very much those of John Adams. In the debates that followed, he played a leading role in defending the document to the Second Continental Congress. When all was said and done, and the document was agreed to, John Adams wrote to his wife, Abigail: "The second day of July 1776 will be the most memorable epoch in the history of America. I am apt to believe that it will be celebrated by succeeding generations as the great anniversary festival. It ought to be commemorated as the Day of Deliverance by solemn acts of devotion to God Almighty. It ought to be solemnized with pomp and parade, with shows, games, sports, guns, bells, bonfires, and illuminations."[9]

All of this did occur and still occurs today. The only difference is that John Adams predicted it would happen on July 2, which was when the delegates

July Second or July Fourth?

There has always been some controversy surrounding these two dates. Which should we celebrate as America's Independence Day?

The delegates of the Continental Congress approved the Declaration of Independence on July 2, 1776. This was the day John Adams meant when he said it should be celebrated in the future with bonfires, bells, sports, and games. John Adams was literally correct; this was the day when our Declaration of Independence came into being.

Today, however, we celebrate our national holiday on July 4.

The Declaration was approved by the delegates on July 2, but it was not signed until July 4. Even then, it was only John Hancock and a few other delegates who actually signed the document on that date. Many of the other delegates did not sign until almost a month later. By then, Americans in every colony knew about the great Declaration. It had been copied very quickly and sent by horse and rider throughout the 13 colonies.

So, although the document was approved on July 2, and although it was not actually signed by all of the delegates until August, it is on July 4 that Americans traditionally celebrate their declaration of independence.

approved the Declaration, but it is July 4, when the leaders of the Second Continental Congress signed the Declaration, that has become the day on which America's independence is traditionally celebrated.

Test Your Knowledge

I What major change took place between the meetings of the First and Second Continental Congresses?
a. George Washington became commander-in-chief of the Continental Army.
b. Thomas Jefferson wrote the Declaration of Independence.
c. The war began between Britain and the American colonies.
d. The British occupied Philadelphia.

2 In 1775, Adams openly criticized a fellow delegate in a letter than was later published. Who was the victim of Adams's criticism?
a. Benjamin Franklin.
b. Thomas Jefferson.
c. John Hancock.
d. John Dickinson.

3 Why did Adams nominate George Washington as commander-in-chief of the Continental Army?
a. He admired Washington's outspoken criticism of the British military.
b. He was impressed by the detailed battle plans Washington presented to the Congress before his nomination.
c. He believed that Washington's appointment would help unify the colonies in the struggle and demonstrate that the conflict was not confined to New England.
d. There were no other obvious candidates for the position.

4 Who first called for the 13 colonies to declare
their independence?
   a. John Adams.
   b. Richard Lee.
   c. Thomas Jefferson.
   d. Benjamin Franklin.

5 Why did Adams predict that July 2 would be the
day on which Americans would celebrate their
independence?
   a. That was the date when all delegates signed
      the Declaration of Independence.
   b. That was the date when the delegates approved
      the Declaration of Independence.
   c. That was the date when Jefferson completed
      his draft of the Declaration of Independence.
   d. That was the date when the Declaration of
      Independence was first debated in the Congress.

ANSWERS: 1. c; 2. d; 3. c; 4. b; 4. b

Man of Diplomacy

The signing of the Declaration of Independence was an important event. The colonies had declared themselves independent states. But they still had to win that independence from Great Britain.

Even as John Adams and his fellow delegates signed the Declaration, the British were launching their greatest effort to date. Admiral Richard Howe and General William Howe brought 30,000 British troops by sea to arrive outside New York City. General George Washington was there to defend New York with about 20,000 men, but they were not trained or seasoned professional soldiers like the British.

John Adams knew how unlikely it was that George Washington could defeat the British at New York. He reluctantly agreed to serve as part of a peace commission. He, Benjamin Franklin, and Edward Rutledge went together to Staten Island, where they met with Admiral Richard Howe.

The admiral was not angry with America or the Americans. He had lost a brother in the French and Indian War. That brother had served with colonial militiamen in upstate New York. Admiral Howe would have liked to end the conflict, but he brought little to offer Adams and the other negotiators. The most Howe would say was that he would recommend to King George that all the rebels be pardoned. There was no talk of American rights or the natural liberties of British subjects.

Adams, Franklin, and Rutledge turned down the limited offer. They returned to Philadelphia and the war resumed.

Things went very badly. The British defeated George Washington and his Continental Army in three places. First, New York City fell. Then the British won a battle at White Plains. Finally, the British captured both Fort Lee and Fort Washington, on different sides of the Hudson River. Soon the Americans were fleeing across New Jersey, with the British army behind them.

This was a very low time for the Patriot cause. John Adams was concerned by the disappointing progress of the war, but he was also worried about his wife and family. He took advantage of one break in the action to return for a short time to Braintree, but most of the time he was in Philadelphia, leading the Board of War.

SURVIVING THE CRISIS

Things got better toward the end of the year. Thomas Paine, who had written *Common Sense* earlier in the year, now wrote *The Crisis*. He urged Americans to stay in the fight, to go through the worst times. Again, Thomas Paine's words came when they were needed most.

On Christmas Day, 1776, George Washington crossed the Delaware River. He attacked the Hessian (German) troops at Trenton and defeated or captured

While Adams served the patriotic cause, Abigail kept him informed of events in Massachusetts. Adams worried about the safety of his family as Minutemen and British troops clashed.

them. This was a major victory at a time that it was desperately needed, and all supporters of the Revolution, from John Adams to the lowest private, felt the difference. There was new life in the American cause.

New challenges and difficulties came with the new year. In 1777, British commanders sent three armies against the Americans. One army came down from Canada. A second came down by way of Lake Ontario. The third, commanded by General William Howe, sailed from New York City to attack Philadelphia.

Philadelphia had been the center of the revolutionary movement since 1774, when the First Continental Congress met there. John Adams and his fellow delegates had become very accustomed to Philadelphia. It was their second home. As the British attacked, the Continental Army tried and failed to stop the British advance. General George Washington lost the Battle of Brandywine Creek, and the British took Philadelphia. The Continental Congress fled the city and went to York, Pennsylvania. It was another low moment for the American cause.

Fortunately, good news soon followed. One of the British armies had had to turn back, and the other one had surrendered at Saratoga, New York. This was the largest American victory to date, and it greatly cheered the delegates to the Continental Congress.

A CHANGE OF PACE

In November 1777, John Adams went home to Massachusetts. He had served for two and a half years and he was ready for a change of pace. He made it home that autumn and was delighted with what he found: a warm, loving family; a snug house; a period of rest after the labors of the past several years. Adams decided that he wanted to return to the practice of law. He was finished with politics and public service.

Adams publicly and privately announced his wish to return to private life. But within two months, he received the news that Congress had named him one of three diplomats to travel to France and persuade the French to support the colonies in their war against Britain.

John Adams had many reasons to turn down the appointment. His wife was terrified of the ocean and did not want to see him leave. He wanted a period of living at home, surrounded by his family. But John Adams was a Patriot and he believed in service to the cause. So, in January 1778, he took ship from Boston and sailed for France. He did not go alone. His oldest son, John Quincy Adams, who was only ten, went with him.

John Adams and John Quincy Adams had a rough voyage. Even though he had lived within sight of the ocean for much of his life, John Adams had never been a fisherman or spent much time on boats. He had been a farmer and a lawyer, a man used to horses, carriages, and walking. Now he had to become used to keeping his feet on deck as the ship pitched and swayed with the waves.

This trip was a wonderful time for young John Quincy Adams. He loved the excitement and learned a great deal by talking to sailors. By the time the trip was over, young John Quincy had learned the names of all the sails and knew a good deal about ocean travel.

Father and son arrived on the west coast of France that spring. By April, John Adams and his son were in Paris.

Adams's first impressions of Paris were of a city nearly overwhelming in its size and beauty. Adams had spent most of his life in a town of less than a thousand people. Philadelphia had seemed enormous with its population of 40,000. In Paris, Adams found himself in a city that was home to half a million people.

Adams was more pleased with Paris than he expected. He had viewed France as an enemy nation, due in part to the French and Indian War. But he came to like many things about Paris and France, especially the politeness of the people.

FORMING AN ALLIANCE

Once he was in Paris, John Adams joined with his two fellow Americans, Benjamin Franklin and Arthur Lee, who were also serving as diplomats to France. Together, the three men were expected to develop an alliance with France and to gain much needed support for the war effort.

As the diplomats began their challenging task, conflict erupted between Adams and Franklin. Adams frankly confessed the difficulties in his letters to Abigail and to friends. Franklin was a great and good man, Adams wrote, but he was past his prime. At the time, Franklin was a little over 70 years old, and he was very careless with money and affairs, something that Adams could not understand or accept.

Adams was also jealous of the overwhelming popularity Franklin experienced in Paris. The French people loved Franklin. They adored his simple clothing and rustic ways. And Franklin loved the glamorous life of the French court, enjoying parties, fine food and fine wine while playing his role as a "simple American."

Military successes made the diplomatic mission's task easier. The French King Louis XVI was very pleased to learn about the British surrender at Saratoga. While unwilling to support a losing cause, he was happy to agree to an alliance with a successful power. He entered the war as an American ally, forcing Britain to fight on two fronts on different sides of the Atlantic Ocean.

John Adams was very pleased with this result. Feeling confident that the mission had been completed, he left France and went home in the autumn of 1778.

Abigail Adams was overjoyed to see her husband and son. She had run the family farm in their absence. She had written dozens of letters to her husband, but many of them had never reached him.

John Adams was delighted to be back home. Once again, he declared his intention to remain in Massachusetts and return to practicing law. But once again, events and the Continental Congress decided otherwise.

DRAFTING A CONSTITUTION

Initially, it was Massachusetts that needed Adams's help. In the summer of 1779, Adams was asked to write a constitution for his home state. This task appealed to him very much. Adams had a powerful, logical mind, and the challenge of drafting a document that would form the basis of government in

Massachusetts inspired him. Within only a few weeks, he had produced a first draft.

Nearly all of Adams's ideas were accepted by the Massachusetts legislature. When the document was finalized, Adams became the author of the first state constitution anywhere in the United States.

In the state's constitution, Adams outlined many of the ideas that had become central to his beliefs about successful government. He favored a legislature made up of two separate bodies. He believed that the British model of the House of Lords and the House of Commons was a good one for the democratic experiment in America. Adams also favored a strong chief executive, a governor who had broad powers in the state government.

Throughout his life, John Adams always claimed that defending the British soldiers in the trial that followed the Boston Massacre was his greatest satisfaction. But many people who study his life and career believe that his contribution in writing the Massachusetts state constitution was his greatest achievement.

When he had completed work on the Massachusetts constitution, a new opportunity for public service appeared—this time again taking him over-seas. In the autumn of 1779, Congress appointed John Adams its minister (ambassador) to Holland. He was to go there by way of France, and to continue to work with Benjamin Franklin to further develop the alliance with France.

Adams was reluctant to leave his home and his country, but he was confident that he could play an important role as a diplomat in Holland. In the autumn of 1779, he and his son, John Quincy, prepared to cross the Atlantic. The crossing was a much rougher voyage than they had experienced on the trip to France, complete with run-ins with British warships. Only good luck—and evasive maneuvers—enabled them to escape capture. The extended journey took them off course, and as a result, they landed on the north coast of Spain, rather than the west coast of France. This meant they had to go nearly 1,000 miles, most of it on mules or by foot, to reach Paris.

When they reached Paris, Adams found a school for John Quincy. In his meetings with Benjamin Franklin, John Adams found that the American cause was at a very low ebb, and the alliance with France in danger of breaking. The French did not believe that the

Americans could win the war against Britain, and there was talk of France seeking a separate peace with England. This was gloomy news, even for someone as stouthearted as John Adams. He went off to Holland, fearing the worst.

AMBASSADOR IN EUROPE

Adams arrived in Holland and was quickly enchanted by the lovely Dutch countryside and the noble Dutch people. But he found it impossible to persuade the Dutch government to listen to his pleas. They did not believe that the Americans could win against Britain, and Adams could not even arrange for a loan from the Dutch government.

John Quincy soon joined him in Holland and was placed in a school there. John Quincy, now 12, showed great promise in his studies. He was an alert, active boy who was willing to learn anything.

Just as Adams was despairing of completing his mission, the American cause rebounded. In 1781, American forces under the command of George Washington trapped the British army at Yorktown, Virginia. A French fleet arrived in time to blockade Chesapeake Bay and prevent the British army's escape.

On October 19, 1781, the British laid down their guns, swords, and cannon at Yorktown. George Washington had won the greatest victory of the war.

As the Americans celebrated the victory, Adams was able to obtain loans from the Dutch. He also learned, by mail, that he had been named as one of the American commissioners to negotiate the peace treaty with Great Britain.

The Battle of Yorktown

Yorktown, Virginia, was a tobacco town, where ships came to load the tobacco grown by local farmers. It was a quiet place until the summer of 1781, when British General Cornwallis brought his army there. He thought he would be safe at Yorktown, since the British navy could re-supply him there.

The British had the finest navy in the world, and this gave them a great advantage while fighting the Continental Army. But, unknown to Cornwallis, the French alliance was about to pay off for America.

In August 1781, George Washington learned that a French fleet was sailing for the Chesapeake Bay. Washington was deeply disappointed, for he wanted to trap the British in New York City and end the war there.

The negotiations took place in Paris. Once again, John Adams worked closely with Benjamin Franklin. The two men found it difficult to agree in private, but they worked well together in public. Together they pressed the British to make major concessions in the peace treaty. When the final treaty was approved, in 1783, it gave the young United States control of most of the land east of the Mississippi River. The

But Washington was supremely adaptable. Moving with great speed, he left a small fighting force outside New York and hastened with most of his troops to Virginia.

The French navy arrived first, and blockaded Cornwallis at Yorktown. Then, George Washington and his troops arrived from the New York area and blocked him in by land. The Battle of Yorktown ended on October 19, 1781, when Cornwallis surrendered his entire army. As the British soldiers marched to lay down their arms, the British bands played the song, "The World Turned Upside Down." It was almost impossible for them to believe that an untrained, undisciplined fighting force had been able to defeat the greatest military power in the world.

Prisoners on both Sides shall be set at Liberty, and His Britannic Majesty shall with all convenient Speed, and without causing any Destruction, or carrying away any Negroes or other Property of the American Inhabitants, withdraw all his Armies, Garrisons and Fleets from the said United States, and from every Post, Place and Harbour within the same: leaving in all Fortifications, the American Artillery that may be therein: And shall also order and cause all Archives, Records, Deeds and Papers belonging to any of the said States or their Citizens, which in the Course of the War may have fallen into the Hands of His officers, to be forthwith restored and delivered to the proper States and Persons to whom they belong.

Article 8th.

The Navigation of the River Mississippi, from its Source to the Ocean, shall for ever remain free and open to the Subjects of Great Britain and the Citizens of the United States.

Article 9th

In Case it should so happen that any Place or Territory belonging to Great Britain or to the United States, should have been conquered by the Arms of either, from the other, before the arrival of the said Provisional Articles in America, it is agreed that the same shall be restored without Difficulty and without requiring any Compensation.

Article

Adams helped negotiate the 1783 Treaty of Paris, which ended the American Revolution and formally recognized the independence of the United States.

Americans also had the right to fish for cod off the Grand Banks. These were major victories for the young country, and John Adams played a major role in winning them. The peace commissioners were painted in a group portrait that showed Adams and Franklin at their best. Together, the thin-skinned man from Massachusetts and the large, expansive man from Pennsylvania had done great things.

Test Your Knowledge

I Why did Adams travel with Benjamin Franklin and Edward Rutledge to Staten Island in 1776?

    a. To negotiate a peace settlement with Admiral Richard Howe.

    b. To meet with Washington and review his battle plans.

    c. To raise funds to support the Continental Army.

    d. None of the above.

2 What happened when British troops invaded Philadelphia?

    a. The Continental Congress was forced to meet in secret.

    b. The Congress dissolved and delegates returned to their homes.

    c. The Congress fled to York, Pennsylvania.

    d. Delegates joined Washington's troops in forcing the British to retreat.

3 Why did Adams travel to France in January 1778?

    a. He wanted to persuade Benjamin Franklin to return to Philadelphia.

    b. He wanted to persuade the French to support the colonies in their war with Britain.

    c. He wanted to persuade the French not to ally themselves with Spain in the war.

    d. He wanted to persuade France to withdraw from North America.

4 What document was Adams asked to write in
the summer of 1779?
a. The Declaration of Independence.
b. The United States Constitution.
c. The Massachusetts Constitution.
d. The Bill of Rights.

5 What terms were contained in the peace treaty
with Britain?
a. The United States gained control of most of
the land east of the Mississippi River.
b. The United States doubled its size, gaining
control of a vast stretch of territory known
as "Louisiana."
c. The United States was awarded vast stretches
of property formerly owned by Loyalists.
d. All of the above.

ANSWERS: 1. a; 2. c; 3. b; 4. c; 5. a

Vice-President
of the
United States

The war was over. The peace treaty was signed. Once more, John Adams made plans to return home. Fate decided otherwise. His country needed him, first as an ambassador to France, and then as the ambassador to Great Britain. Once again, John Adams agreed to do what was best for his country.

This time, however, Adams was not alone. His beloved Abigail sailed from Massachusetts in 1784. She joined him in Paris, and then the two of them traveled together to London. While they were in Paris, John and Abigail Adams enjoyed the company of Thomas Jefferson. Since writing the Declaration of Independence, the Virginian had served as governor of his home state. Now he was in Paris, replacing Adams as the American ambassador to France while Adams took up his post in London.

John and Abigail Adams arrived in London in May 1785. As much as he hated British tyranny and as long as he had fought the British, John Adams could not help but admire London. This was the center of the English-speaking world. London was home to a million people. The great dome of St. Paul's Cathedral stood out as one of the architectural wonders of the time. Adams was impressed by the evidence that, despite its defeat in America, the British Empire was still flourishing.

John Adams met King George III on June 1, 1785. This was an historic meeting, the first official diplomatic meeting between an American ambassador and the British king.

John Adams went in slowly. His hands shook. He was nearly overcome by emotion. There, seated in front of him, was King George III, whom Thomas Jefferson had once described as a "royal brute." Adams had fought this man for the past ten years. He had worked against him in Paris, in Holland, and in his native America. Now he stood before him.

Despite the importance of the moment, Adams was not at a loss for words. "I think myself more fortunate than all my fellow-citizens," he said, "in having the distinguished honor to be the first to stand in your Majesty's royal presence in a diplomatic character; and I shall esteem myself the happiest of men if I can be instrumental in recommending my country more and more to your Majesty's royal benevolence." [10]

For a moment, there was silence as all those present waited for the king's response. When it finally came, it was clear that Adams's words had been well chosen.

"I will be very frank with you," King George III said. "I was the last to consent to separation; but the separation having been made, and having become inevitable, I have always said, as I say now, that I would be the first to meet the friendship of the United States as an independent power." [11]

DIFFICULT YEARS IN LONDON

John and Abigail Adams spent the next three years in London. They were not very happy there. King George and Queen Charlotte were almost always polite, but the British people treated the couple with hostility. British newspapers said it was absurd to have an American ambassador to Britain when it was likely that the American states would come back to England on their own. Many in England (and throughout Europe) shared this view, believing that the United States was spread out over too great a landmass, that its people would need the safety and security of belonging to England once more. No republic or democracy of the size of the United States had yet succeeded. In fact, it had never been tried before.

While John Adams was in London and while Thomas Jefferson was in Paris, other American leaders were at work shaping the new government. In 1786, farmers in western Massachusetts rose up in what became known as Shays' Rebellion. The rebellion frightened American leaders enough that they gathered in Philadelphia in 1787 and wrote a new Constitution for the United States.

The document established a strong federal government but left many powers to the individual state governments. Even though he was not completely pleased with the result, John Adams believed that this was as good a constitution as could be created in the short time (four months) that the delegates had been given.

The new constitution was welcome news, but even better was to come. In December 1787, Adams learned that he had been relieved of his assignment as ambassador. In the summer of 1788, he, Abigail, and their children returned home to Braintree, Massachusetts. They arrived to a thunderous welcome. Governor John Hancock arranged it so that the cannon of Boston fired a major salute to John Adams as he returned home. In the past ten years, he had spent nearly nine years abroad, all of them in the service of his beloved country.

A NEW ROLE

Adams arrived home to learn that the new constitution had been approved by the individual states. The United States now had a federal government, based in New York City. Adams was about to settle into his life in Braintree when he learned that people wanted him to serve as Vice-President of the United States.

John Adams was not well suited for the vice-presidency. He had spent so many years as his own man, whether it was as a lawyer, farmer, congressman, or diplomat, that it seemed unfair for him to take a secondary role in any situation. But Adams was asked and encouraged by his friends. They told him he could do more good as vice-president than in any other capacity.

There was no question of becoming president. Everyone knew that George Washington would be selected as the first president of the United States. His stature was so great that it could not be otherwise.

There was no popular vote, no direct election by the people. The first nine elections for president and vice-president were done strictly by the members of the Electoral College. John Adams did not have to campaign for the post of vice-president. He simply had to say that he was interested, and the electors would decide if they wanted him.

In the end, George Washington won the first presidential election by a unanimous vote, while John Adams won a rather narrow majority of votes for vice-president. This was not very pleasing to Adams, but he saw his duty and went to New York City, the first capital of the United States. On April 30, 1789,

George Washington was inaugurated as the nation's
first president in 1789. John Adams became the first
vice-president.

George Washington was sworn in as the nation's first president and John Adams became the country's first vice-president.

A QUESTION OF TITLES

When they took office, George Washington and John Adams were new leaders of a new nation. They knew that this could be tricky. Both men wanted to smooth the way for the people who would follow them. They did this by setting precedents.

John Adams got into trouble very early in his vice-presidency. It was agreed that the vice-president would preside over the United States Senate and that he would cast the deciding vote if the Senate votes were tied. But how should he, and the president, be addressed?

All of his life, John Adams had been a man of the people. He had fought Britain and what he viewed as tyranny. He had fought for the rights of the common man. But having spent many years in Europe, Adams had been influenced by the formality and grandeur of the governments there. He felt that it was important for the new nation to adopt some of the same customs, to ensure that its leaders would be viewed with the same respect as the rulers of Europe. John Adams wasted weeks in the Senate debating the question of what the president should be called. Should he be "Your Excellency?" "Sir?" No one seemed quite sure.

John Adams pushed for a more formal term of address. Observers heaped scorn on him and brought up the charge that he was really a monarchist (a supporter of rule by a monarch or king) at heart. Pointing to Adams's weight and size, people began to call him "His Rotundity." [12]

The matter was finally settled by the president. George Washington would be called "President of the United States." No other title was necessary. But this flap over the matter of titles cost Adams. His reputation was tarnished because he had wasted important time over a trivial issue, and people never let him forget it.

As vice-president, Adams was overshadowed by two other members of the administration. His old friend, Thomas Jefferson, became secretary of state, and Alexander Hamilton became secretary of the treasury. These two men became George Washington's leading advisers, while Adams played a secondary role, focusing instead on attending every session of the Senate.

Adams served with his friend Thomas Jefferson (shown above), who was Washington's secretary of state. Their friendship was tested by events in America and France.

Abigail and the rest of the family moved to New York City to be with Adams. For the first time in many years, they enjoyed a comfortable lifestyle.

When the federal government was moved from New York City to Philadelphia, both John and Abigail regretted the move, as they had been very happy in New York.

REVOLUTION IN FRANCE

The French Revolution began in the summer of 1789, just two months after Adams became vice-president. At first, events in France seemed to mimic the events that

The Guillotine

Today, the word *guillotine* conjures up gory images of a sharp blade slicing through skin and bone. But the guillotine was invented by a Frenchman who thought it would be a tool used for good, since executions would be made swifter and cause less suffering.

In medieval times, executions often involved the command, "Off with his head." When this sentence was pronounced, the victim's head was removed with a heavy axe. Even the best executioner found it difficult to accurately place the axe's blade, and it often required two blows, or sometimes three, to finish the job. Shortly before the French Revolution began, a Frenchman named Guillotin invented a new system for execution: a more had marked the beginning of the American Revolution. The early part of the French Revolution was a dignified affair. King Louis XVI remained as king, but with limited powers. The French appointed a legislature, known as the National Assembly, and issued a Declaration of the Rights of Man and the Citizen.

Adams was one of the first to sense that the French Revolution would not proceed in as peaceful a manner as it had begun. While approving of the initial steps

accurate instrument that would only need one strike to finish the job.

Named for its inventor, the guillotine was an instrument with a sharp blade raised many feet in the air. At a signal, a man moved a lever and the sharp blade came crashing down, slicing off the person's head. This instrument was made to ensure that a person's head came off the first time. The perhaps unintended result was that executions were no longer dependent on the physical strength of a single executioner. The guillotine made it possible for the French revolutionary government to execute hundreds, even thousands, of people in a very short time.

taken by the new government, Adams seemed keenly aware of what might follow.

Sharing the same suspicions about the events in France, Alexander Hamilton and Adams became closer political allies. This placed them in sharp opposition to Thomas Jefferson, who was an outspoken supporter of the French Revolution.

It was Adams and Hamilton who would be proven correct. In 1793, revolutionaries in France beheaded both King Louis XVI and Queen Marie Antoinette. They went further, arresting and beheading many noble men and women. The revolutionaries used a new instrument, called the guillotine, to accomplish this dreadful work.

Adams and Hamilton were now firmly opposed to the French Revolution. While Jefferson was alarmed at the reports of violence and bloodshed, he continued to argue in favor of the French revolutionary cause. During this time of anxiety and fear, the United States government suffered from another problem: an outbreak of yellow fever.

The summer of 1794 brought the worst attack of yellow fever yet seen in the United States. Hundreds of people died. Many others were hospitalized. John and

Abigail Adams were fortunate. They did not contract yellow fever. But they saw many of their friends die, and they became more committed than ever to the cause of public health. Their good friend, Doctor Benjamin Rush, was one of the leaders in the fight against yellow fever.

Disagreements within Washington's cabinet and the fear sparked by the outbreak of yellow fever made Adams's service even more challenging. By 1796, George Washington had completed his second term as president of the United States and announced that he would retire to his beloved home of Mount Vernon in Virginia. Public speculation began to mount over who would succeed Washington as the nation's second president.

Adams wanted the job. He believed that he had the necessary skills, the diplomatic experience, and the knowledge of government, to make him the best candidate. He was not very popular in Philadelphia, but he was well known and his service to his country made him a strong candidate.

The Electoral College awarded John Adams the presidency in 1796. In March 1797, he became the second president of the United States.

Test Your Knowledge

1 Who replaced Adams as ambassador to France when Adams left to become the American ambassador to Britain?

a. Benjamin Franklin.

b. John Paul Jones.

c. Thomas Jefferson.

d. Alexander Hamilton.

2 Why was the meeting between John Adams and King George III on June 1, 1785, considered historic?

a. It was the first time King George III had met an American colonist.

b. It was the first diplomatic meeting between an American ambassador and the British king.

c. Adams refused to bow or kneel before the British king.

d. It was the first time King George III admitted that Britain had lost the war.

3 Which city was the first capital of the United States?

a. Washington, D.C.

b. Philadelphia.

c. Boston.

d. New York City.

4 What was Adams's view of the French Revolution?

a. He supported the revolutionaries, believing that they had much in common with Americans who had fought for their independence.

b. He predicted that the French Revolution would be marked by violence and bloodshed.

c. He opposed the revolution, believing that King Louis XVI and Queen Marie Antoinette were the rightful rulers of France.

d. None of the above.

5 What illness swept across America in the summer of 1794?

a. Influenza.

b. Malaria.

c. Yellow fever.

d. Tuberculosis.

ANSWERS: 1. c; 2. b; 3. d; 4. b; 5. c

President
of the
United States

As the new president, Adams assumed the leadership of a nation in crisis. The country, once unified in opposition to Great Britain, was now divided.

In 1797, the year Adams took office, many Americans were in conflict. Two political factions, or parties, had sprung up from the divisions that had marked Washington's

Adams was elected president in 1796. He served as the nation's second president for four years.

Cabinet. There were the Federalists, led by John Adams and Alexander Hamilton, and the Anti-Federalists (also called the Republicans) led by Thomas Jefferson.

While Adams and Jefferson were bitterly divided in their views of how America should be governed, they were forced to work together on a daily basis. Under the complicated election system of those days, the person who received the second highest number of electoral votes (the runner-up) became vice-president. In the election of 1796, Jefferson had received slightly fewer votes than Adams, so despite their deep differences, Jefferson became Adams's vice-president.

Adams and Jefferson had been the best of friends during the period when Adams was the ambassador to London and Jefferson the ambassador to Paris. The Adams and Jefferson families had met often, exchanged gifts, and even considered a marriage between one of the Adams sons and a Jefferson daughter. But all that was now past, and Adams and Jefferson had become political enemies, divided by their very different views on how American should be governed.

The Federalists believed in a powerful federal government. The Anti-Federalists believed in states' rights and a federal government of weak to moderate strength.

When he took office, Adams believed that it would be his task to unite the country. But opposition to him continued, sparked in part by the ongoing debate over the proper role for America in the French Revolution.

THE X, Y, Z AFFAIR

The French Revolution had begun in 1789 and in 1797 it was still continuing on its murderous path. The guillotine had stopped doing its bloody work and people were no longer being beheaded. But the French Revolutionary armies were fighting Britain, Spain, Austria, and Prussia. The French wanted the United States to come to their aid. Had they not done so for the Americans during their Revolution?

As President, John Adams wanted to stay out of the war caused by the French Revolution. He wanted to follow in the wise course laid down by President George Washington, who had declared American neutrality in the European conflict. Then, in 1797, Adams learned that French ships-of-war were attacking and taking American merchant ships in the Caribbean. This had to stop. Adams sent three men across the ocean to negotiate a new treaty with France.

The three commissioners were John Marshall, Charles Pinckney, and Elbridge Gerry. Adams knew and trusted all three of them. The three men made the ocean crossing and arrived in Paris. They asked to meet with the French Foreign Minister, Count Talleyrand.

To their surprise, the three Americans were greeted by three Frenchmen, none of whom was a minister or ambassador. These three Frenchmen hinted that a bribe or gift of money was necessary in order to meet with Count Talleyrand. This was simply unheard of, and so the three Americans asked the three Frenchmen to repeat themselves. They were told again that money would need to be offered before they could meet with the top French diplomat. The amount suggested was around $250,000, an astonishing amount at a time when the entire United States budget was only a few million dollars.

Charles Pinckney, from South Carolina, gave the answer, "No, no, not a sixpence." This answer was later repeated in the United States and was changed into a rallying cry: "Millions for defense but not one penny for tribute!"[13]

The three Americans quickly wrote their account of what had happened and sent it to President Adams.

To protect the identity of the three Frenchmen involv-ed, the three Americans identified them simply as Monsieurs X, Y, and Z.

Adams received the news with astonishment. Like his three diplomats, he could hardly believe that the French Revolutionary government would be so ridiculous and so aggressive. Meanwhile, French ships continued to attack and seize American ships on the high seas.

BUILDING A NAVY

Even before he learned of the demands of Monsieurs X, Y, and Z, Adams had put the small American navy on a war footing. During the administration of George Washington, the nation had taken on the task of building seven new frigates for the American navy. These ships, which carried between 40 and 50 guns, were built in Boston, Newport, New York, Philadelphia, Baltimore, Portsmouth, and Charleston. John Adams was especially proud when Boston launched its 44-gun ship, named the U.S.S. *Constitution* (later it would gain the nickname "Old Ironsides").

The new ships came off the docks in 1797 and 1798. Adams had a powerful force with which he could strike at the French. He decided to use this new naval power, but not to use the United States army. As much as he hated what the French had done in the X, Y, Z Affair, Adams wanted to hold back from a full-scale war.

In 1798, with the country fully behind him, Adams renounced the treaties of alliance with France. These treaties dated back to 1778, the year in which John Adams had first gone to France, many of them treaties he himself had helped negotiate.

The new American frigates were sent to patrol in the Caribbean, and they quickly engaged in battles with French frigates. The Americans won most of the ship-to-ship battles. Americans were thrilled with the victories, and elated that their new navy was showing such skill.

John Adams was now at the peak of his popularity. He could easily have increased his popularity and even insured his re-election in 1800 by declaring a full-scale war against France. But to do so would put the nation at risk, and Adams believed that he was accomplishing what he needed to through the show of naval force. He held back from a full-scale declaration of war.

This decision, made for the security of America, caused many to despise Adams. He was branded a coward and unpatriotic. His popularity began to slip.

Matters grew worse when Adams signed two Acts of Congress that would become the most controversial the young nation had yet seen. The Alien Act required that all foreigners register with the United States government. If a foreigner had been in the country for less than seven years, the president could deport him without any trial. The Sedition Act made it illegal for newspapers to print any material directly critical of the United States government. Newspaper editors and newspaper owners could be fined or even imprisoned for printing articles critical of the president or any government official.

John Adams had not requested Congress to pass these acts. But he signed them, making them into law. The Alien Act was seldom used, but the Sedition Act was used and a number of journalists were put into prison for writing articles critical of the federal government, inspiring many to accuse Adams and his administration of censorship.

Adams was now in a difficult place, forced to represent and even defend the positions of the Federalist

Party. Adams became the focus for all criticism of Federalist policies and positions, and he quickly became one of the most unpopular political figures in the country.

A NEW HOME

In 1800, John and Abigail Adams moved from

The White House

John and Abigail Adams were the first presidential couple to live in the White House. It did not carry that name yet; instead, it was known as the President's House.

The capital of the United States was in New York from 1789 until 1792, and in Philadelphia from 1792 until 1800. In those years, George Washington and a French engineer, Pierre L'Enfant, laid out what later became Washington and the District of Columbia. The president and L'Enfant wanted Washington to be a planned city, rather than one that grew up by fits and starts. As a result, the streets of Washington make excellent sense even today, for they were built wide enough so that many carriages (and now many cars) could move easily.

John and Abigail Adams moved into the new President's House, but they found it had not been properly furnished.

Philadelphia to Washington, D.C. They were the first couple to live in the new "President's House," the presidential mansion that has served as the home for all presidents in the years that followed. The president and his wife were not thrilled by the move. Washington was a small, muddy town, far removed from the centers of power. It would take years of

Both John and Abigail were very practical and frugal, and, knowing that Adams might not be re-elected, they decided not to spend much money on this new home. Abigail hung her laundry out to dry in the large East Wing of the President's House.

As things turned out, they were wise not to spend too much on furniture or decorations, since Adams lost the election of 1800. They left the President's House in 1801 and never returned.

The President's House became nearer and dearer to many Americans in the War of 1812. The British captured Washington, D.C., and occupied it for one day in the summer of 1814. The British burned many buildings, including the President's House. Because it was made of stone and wood, much of the President's House endured even after the new White House was built.

building and improvements before it would become the great capital city that we know today.

That same year, Adams ran for re-election. He was opposed by Vice-President Jefferson and by two other men, Aaron Burr and Alexander Hamilton.

Adams did not make a strong bid for re-election. He knew that it was unlikely, he knew that he was unpopular, and he was ready to go home to Braintree, Massachusetts. But he still felt bitter that, after so many years of faithful service to his country, the country seemed so eager to replace him.

Adams came in fourth in the ballots of the Electoral College. He was not re-elected.

Thomas Jefferson and Aaron Burr tied for first place. This threw the election into the United States House of Representatives. The run-off election was held there, and Thomas Jefferson was elected the third president of the United States.

On March 4, 1801, John and Abigail Adams left Washington, D.C., in a carriage. They left early in the morning to avoid the inaugural ceremony held for Thomas Jefferson.

Test Your Knowledge

1 Which were the first two political parties in the United States?

   a. The Democratic Party and the Republican Party.

   b. The Republican Party and the Whig Party.

   c. The Federalist Party and the Anti-Federalist Party.

   d. The Patriot Party and the Loyalist Party.

2 During John Adams's presidency, who served as vice-president?

   a. Thomas Jefferson.

   b. Alexander Hamilton.

   c. James Madison.

   d. George Taylor.

3 What political ideal did the Federalists support?

   a. Powerful states with strong rights, and a weak to moderate central government.

   b. A strong and powerful national government.

   c. Proportional representation, based on a state's population and geographical size.

   d. None of the above.

4 What was the X, Y, Z Affair?

   a. A scandal involving Adams's son, John Quincy, and allegations that he had accepted bribes.

   b. An argument between Alexander Hamilton and Aaron Burr that ended in a duel.

   c. A disastrous battle between the French and American navies.

   d. A scandal in which bribes were demanded of American commissioners attempting to negotiate a treaty with France.

5 John and Abigail Adams were the first presidential couple to:

   a. Have a child during his presidency.

   b. Engage in a political campaign.

   c. Live in the White House, which was then called the President's House.

   d. Give interviews to journalists.

ANSWERS: 1. c; 2. a; 3. b; 4. d; 5. c

Retirement
and
Reconciliation

John and Abigail Adams arrived home in March 1801. They were home to stay. They had suffered private, as well as public, loss. In 1800, the same year that he lost the presidential election, Adams lost his second son, Charles.

Charles Adams had always been a winning boy, a good student, and beloved by his parents. But his behavior was often self-destructive. By the time he died in 1800, Charles Adams was an alcoholic who had never lived up to his potential. This was very sad for Adams, and he and Abigail lamented the loss of their son.

At the same time, their oldest son was turning out to be more and more of a success. John Quincy Adams had been only ten when his father took him to France in 1778. Since then, John Quincy had learned several languages, had served as his father's confidential secretary, and become a man of great promise. John Quincy Adams soon ran for and was elected to the U.S. House of Representatives.

With so much good around him, John Adams could be content. He had done his life's work with skill and dedication. He could now relax and watch his grandchildren grow up around him.

Adams kept an eye on the political scene, too. He no longer participated in politics, but he was interested in them.

Thomas Jefferson, who had been both his friend and his enemy, was now president. Under Jefferson, the nation doubled its size by buying the Louisiana area from France. "Louisiana" meant much more than the current state of Louisiana. It meant the

John Adams's oldest son, John Quincy, enjoyed a successful political career, becoming the sixth president of the United States.

whole area between the Mississippi River and the Rocky Mountains.

Adams had to admit that Jefferson was doing rather well as president. But by 1805, Jefferson was encountering difficulties in his presidency, difficulties with which Adams could easily relate. This time it was British ships-of-war that stole American sailors from their ships.

At one point, Jefferson announced that no American ships could leave American ports carrying any cargo. Jefferson thought this might stop the British actions, but his effort failed.

By the time his second term as president was up, in 1809, Jefferson was very ready to leave public life. Like Adams, Jefferson had found the presidency a difficult, demanding job.

PEACEMAKING BY POST

In retirement, Adams wrote letters to his many friends from different parts of the United States. One of his oldest and best friends was Benjamin Rush. Rush was a doctor who had served in the Continental Congress with Adams. Rush had worked to fight the yellow fever epidemic in Philadelphia in 1794. He and Adams were great friends, and they exchanged many letters. In one, Rush told Adams that he had had a dream—a dream in which he saw Adams write a letter to Jefferson, in order to resume their friendship. In the dream, Jefferson

losophers about universal and perpetual Peace, as Short Sighted frivolous
Romances.

"Your Reflection in your Yard of Insanity, reminds me of mine in
the Royal Menagerie at Versailles viz: "What Should a Man Say to this
"Assembly of Birds and Beasts if he had thoughts of recommending to them
"the Institution of a Republican Government by universal Suffrage." Just
the Same as he could rationally Say to the Same number of Frenchmen taken
at random or by Choice from the Court the City the Country, the Army, the Navy
the Merchants, Tradesmen Farmers, or the Sorbon or the Church. The Project
of a Republican Government in France was often Suggested in conversation
even then and occupied much of thought during the whole time I was in that
Country.

In my Letter of the 3 of this month I have corrected a Mistake of your
Pen or Memory. It was Hillsborough not Grenville who expressed the Jealousy
of American Canvas and Sails.

I have not calculated with precision enough yet, to resolve the Theorem
Whether the Banking Capital does not exceed the Value of the Fee Simple
of the United States.

The Sunday before last I went, the next Town to Church, our Minister
having gone to the Funeral of his Brother. A Mr Shelden, the occasional Preacher
One of our ardent Spirits in Pulpit oratory told Us "that "Awakenings," and
"Revivals" produced great divisions in Society. They Set Fathers against
Sons, Mothers against Daughters, Brothers against Brothers, Sisters
against Sisters, Neighbour against Neighbour and Friend against
Friend.

Wars do as much of this as Revivals or Awakenings, and I believe
as innocently and piously. Your Family is peculiarly Situated: but I
doubt not every Branch of it will perform its duty with honor and Integrity.
Our Massachusetts and Connecticut are a little out of humour and
and Pensilvania
are retaliating upon Virginia, in 1798 Somewhat grossly: but the little Eddy
in the Atmosphere will dissipate and whirl away. A Vote to build a few
Frigates would blow it off at once.

I have made my Sons and Daughters Sing "There is no Comfort
in the Hills when my good Girls avoa" these thirty years. It is one of the best
Morsels of Poetry that ever was conceived

Dr Rush,   Adieu
                                            John Adams

Adams kept in touch with friends by writing lengthy,
thoughtful letters like this one to Benjamin Rush, a doctor
who had served in the Continental Congress with Adams.
Rush later urged Adams to renew his friendship with
Thomas Jefferson.

wrote back, and the two former friends and former enemies had become friends once more.

Adams did not immediately respond to Rush's letter. He had very painful and mixed feelings about Jefferson. Adams did not even know that his wife Abigail had written to Jefferson on her own, seeking to reestablish what had once been their friendship. This attempt to rebuild from the past had failed, even though Jefferson had indeed responded to her letter.

Wounds take time to heal. No one can really predict when a person will be ready to make the first move toward reconciliation. But we do know that Adams went ahead. On January 1, 1812, he wrote a short letter to Jefferson. This was their first correspondence, in any form, since the year 1801.

Jefferson wrote back very soon. He, too, had not forgotten how much they had shared in the early days of their struggle for independence. He, too, remembered how much they had done together when they were diplomats aboard. And, like Adams, Jefferson made it a point not to bring up the painful time from the 1790s when the two men were political foes. Jefferson wrote, "Of the signers of the Declaration of Independence, I see now not living more than half a dozen on your side of the Potomac [River], and on this side myself alone. You and I have been wonderfully spared, and myself with remarkable health and a considerable activity of body and mind." [14]

Benjamin Rush had helped to bring about this reconciliation. In 1812, he sent to Adams his first copy of *Medical Inquiries and Observations upon the Diseases of the Mind*. This important book was one of the early milestones in the road toward an understanding of the field of mental health.

Benjamin Rush died in 1813. Adams was very sad, since another link with his past was now broken. Other friends died, too. Then, in 1818, Adams lost his beloved Abigail. His dear friend, his essential helper and mate, was gone. She died at the age of 74.

Abigail Adams died when her son, John Quincy, had become secretary of state. She did not have the joy of seeing him become president of the United States, since he was elected to that office in 1824. But John Adams was still alive. Until the year 2001, when George W. Bush became the forty-third president of the United States, John Adams and John Quincy Adams were the only father-son pair ever to hold the highest office in the land.

A FINAL FOURTH

In the last two years of life, John Adams was very sick. His hands shook and he could no longer do the four-mile walks that had once been his custom. But he was not alone or isolated. People came from far and wide to see him. At the age of 90, he was one of the few survivors from the early American Revolutionary group.

In the spring of 1826, John Adams was keenly aware that it would soon be the fiftieth anniversary of the Declaration of Independence. He wanted to make it to that date, as a milestone for his life and career.

In that same spring, Thomas Jefferson was still alive at his home of Monticello in Virginia. He, too, understood the significance of the July 4 date.

Both men did survive to witness the fiftieth anniversary of the document they had created, the document that would dramatically transform their nation. John Adams died in the afternoon. His last words were "Thomas Jefferson still survives." In truth, Thomas Jefferson died that same day. Both men died on the afternoon of July 4, 1826. In all of American history, there has never been a more symbolic moment of passage for two great leaders and men.

LEGACY OF A LEADER

John Adams was gone, at the ripe age of 91. What was his legacy?

He died knowing that the nation he had helped create was firmly on its feet. In 1826, there was no question that the United States would survive. The only question was: To what extent would it thrive?

John Adams died knowing that the values he believed in were secure. He had always believed in work, discipline, and public service. These values were very much part of the social fabric of America when he died.

Finally, John Adams died knowing that the Adams family would last long after him. He had always been proud of being descended from humble, honest, and hardworking people. Now, his descendants would be proud of being descended from the second president of the United States.

Test Your Knowledge

I What positions did John Quincy Adams hold in his lifetime?

　　a. President of the United States.

　　b. Member of the House of Representatives.

　　c. Confidential secretary to his father.

　　d. All of the above.

2 Who was Benjamin Rush?

　　a. Adams's personal secretary.

　　b. A doctor who had served with Adams in the Continental Congress.

　　c. Vice-president during the presidency of Thomas Jefferson.

　　d. A candidate for the presidency in the election of 1800.

3 In 1812, Adams contacted an old friend, bringing an end to years of public and private quarreling. Who was it?

　　a. George Washington.

　　b. Benjamin Franklin.

　　c. Thomas Jefferson.

　　d. Alexander Hamilton.

4 John Adams and John Quincy Adams were the first father-son pair to become president of the United States. Which other father-son pair achieved this honor?

a. John F. Kennedy and Robert Kennedy.

b. Theodore Roosevelt and Franklin D. Roosevelt.

c. George H.W. Bush and George W. Bush.

d. At no other time have both father and son become president of the United States.

5 Both John Adams and Thomas Jefferson died on July 4, 1826. What other event made that date significant?

a. It was the fiftieth anniversary of the signing of the Declaration of Independence.

b. Both men had also been born on July 4.

c. It was also the date on which George Washington died.

d. It was the first time that July 4 was celebrated as a national holiday.

ANSWERS: 1. d; 2. b; 3. c; 4. c; 5. a

1735 John Adams is born.

1744 Abigail Smith is born.

1755 John Adams graduates from Harvard College; French and Indian War begins.

1761 James Otis protests against new British laws.

1764 John Adams marries Abigail Smith.

1765 Their first child is born.

1765 The Stamp Act takes effect in the American colonies.

1766 The Stamp Act is repealed.

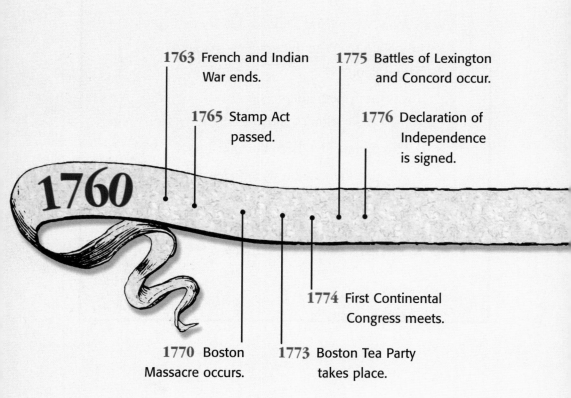

1763 French and Indian War ends.

1775 Battles of Lexington and Concord occur.

1765 Stamp Act passed.

1776 Declaration of Independence is signed.

1760

1774 First Continental Congress meets.

1770 Boston Massacre occurs.

1773 Boston Tea Party takes place.

1768 The Adams family moves to Boston as British regiments arrive in the city.

1770 The Boston Massacre occurs; Adams defends British soldiers accused of murder.

1773 The Boston Tea Party takes place.

1774 The First Continental Congress meets in Philadelphia.

1775 The Battles of Lexington and Concord occur; Second Continental Congress meets.

1776 *Common Sense* published; the Declaration of Independence is signed.

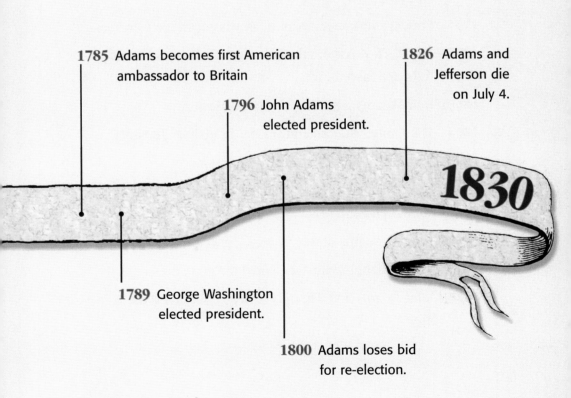

1785 Adams becomes first American ambassador to Britain

1796 John Adams elected president.

1826 Adams and Jefferson die on July 4.

1830

1789 George Washington elected president.

1800 Adams loses bid for re-election.

1778 John Adams travels to France.

1781 George Washington's troops win the Battle of Yorktown.

1785 John Adams travels to Britain as the first American ambassador.

1787 The new Constitution is written.

1789 John Adams becomes the first vice-president; French Revolution begins.

1794 The yellow fever epidemic cripples Philadelphia and other American cities.

1796 John Adams is elected the second president of the United States.

1797 French ships attack American vessels in the Caribbean.

1798 The X, Y, Z Affair takes place; the Alien and Sedition Acts are passed.

1800 John Adams loses his bid for re-election.

1804 The United States acquires the Louisiana Territory.

1809 Thomas Jefferson leaves office.

1812 John Adams writes to Thomas Jefferson, resuming their friendship.

1818 Abigail Adams dies.

1824 John Quincy Adams is elected the sixth president.

1826 John Adams and Thomas Jefferson both die on July 4.

Notes

CHAPTER 1
The Trial

1. David McCullough, *John Adams* (New York: Simon & Schuster, 2001), 68.

CHAPTER 2
Yankee Youth

2. Lynne Withey, *Dearest Friend: A Life of Abigail Adams* (New York: The Free Press, 1981), 21.

CHAPTER 3
Young Revolutionary

3. Attributed to James Otis. Quoted in John Bartlett, *Familiar Quotations* (Boston: Little Brown and Company, 1980), 367.
4. Quoted in McCullough, 60.
5. Quoted in Page Smith, *John Adams* (New York: Doubleday & Company, 1962), 148.
6. Quoted in Benson Bobrick, *Angel in the Whirlwind: The Triumph of the American* Revolution (New York: Simon and Schuster, 1997), 116.

CHAPTER 4
Leading the Way to Independence

7. Quoted in McCullough, 95.
8. Ibid., 104.

9. L.H. Butterfield, ed., *Adams Family Correspondence*, Volume II (Boston: Harvard University Press, 1963), 30.

CHAPTER 6
Vice-President of the United States

10. Quoted in McCullough, 336.
11. Ibid.
12. Lynne Withey, *Dearest Friend: A Life of Abigail Adams* (New York: The Free Press, 1981), 212.

CHAPTER 7
President of the United States

13. Attributed to Robert Goodloe Harper. Quoted in John Bartlett, *Familiar Quotations*, 15th edition (Boston: Little Brown and Company, 1980), 416.

CHAPTER 8
Retirement and Reconciliation

14. Paul Wilstach, ed., *Correspondence of John Adams and Thomas Jefferson* (Indianapolis: Bobbs-Merrill Company, 1925), 34.

Bibliography

Bobrick, Benson. *Angel in the Whirlwind: The Triumph of the American Revolution.* New York: Simon and Schuster, 1997.

McCullough, David. *John Adams.* New York: Simon and Schuster, 2001.

Smith, Page. *John Adams.* New York: Doubleday & Company, 1962.

Wilstach, Paul, ed. *Correspondence of John Adams and Thomas Jefferson.* Indianapolis: Bobbs-Merrill Company, 1925.

Withey, Lynne. *Dearest Friend: A Life of Abigail Adams.* New York: The Free Press, 1981.

Behrman, Carol H. *John Adams*. Minneapolis, Minn.: Lerner
Publications, 2004.

Feinstein, Stephen. *John Adams*. Berkeley Heights, N.J.:
MyReportLinks.com., 2002.

Marcovitz, Hal. *John Adams*. Philadelphia: Mason Crest, 2003.

Santella, Andrew. *John Adams*. Minneapolis, Minn.: Compass Point
Books, 2003.

WEBSITES
Colonial Hall
www.colonialhall.com/adamsj/adamsj.asp

Internet Public Library
www.ipl.org/div/potus/

White House Presidential Biographies
www.whitehouse.gov/history/presidents/ja6.html

Index

Index

Index

SAMUEL WILLARD CROMPTON lives in the hills of western Massachusetts. He is the author or editor of many biographies and history books. He has a long-held interest in the Revolutionary period, which began when his father unearthed a bayonet in the family garden. Crompton teaches history at Holyoke Community College. He is also a contributor to the *American National Biography*, published by Oxford University Press.